Look Inside a

Burrow

Richard Spilsbury

LIBRARY

Chicago, Illinois

Edited by Rebecca Rissman, Dan Nunn, and John-Paul Wilkins
Designed by Steve Mead
Original illustrations © Capstone Global Library Ltd 2013
Illustrations by Gary Hanna
Picture research by Ruth Blair
Production by Alison Parsons
Originated by Capstone Global Library Ltd
Printed in China

16 15 14 13 12
10 9 8 7 6 5 4 3 2 1

Library of Congress Cataloging-in-Publication Data
Spilsbury, Richard, 1963-
  Burrow / Richard Spilsbury.—1st ed.
    p. cm.—(Look inside)
  Includes bibliographical references and index.
  ISBN 978-1-4329-7193-9 (hb)—ISBN 978-1-4329-7200-4 (pb)
1. Burrowing animals—Juvenile literature. 2. Burrower bugs—
Juvenile literature. 3. Niche (Ecology)—Juvenile literature. I. Title.

QL756.15.S65 2013
591.56'48—dc23   2012011713

Acknowledgments
We would like to thank the following for permission to reproduce
photographs: Naturepl pp. 9 (© Andy Sands), 11 (© Kim Taylor),
18 (© Premaphotos), 19 (© Meul / ARCO), 20 (© Artur Tabor),
21 (© George McCarthy), 25 (© Solvin Zankl), 26 (© Terry
Andrewartha), 27 (© Jane Burton); Photoshot p. 17 (© NHPA);
Shutterstock pp. 5 (© Cheryl A. Meyer), 6 (© jack53), 7 (©
Geoffrey Kuchera), 8 (© kurt_G), 12 (© AlexGul), 13 (© t0di),
14 (© xpixel), 15 (© fotosutra.com), 23 (© Pakhnyushcha), 24
(© Tramper), 29 (© Darrell J. Rohl); Superstock p. 28 (© age
footstock).

Cover photograph of field vole (*Microtus agrestis*) eating root,
reproduced with permission of Shutterstock (© CreativeNature.nl).

We would like to thank Michael Bright and Diana Bentley for their
invaluable help in the preparation of this book.

Every effort has been made to contact copyright holders of any
material reproduced in this book. Any omissions will be rectified
in subsequent printings if notice is given to the publisher.

Disclaimer

Contents

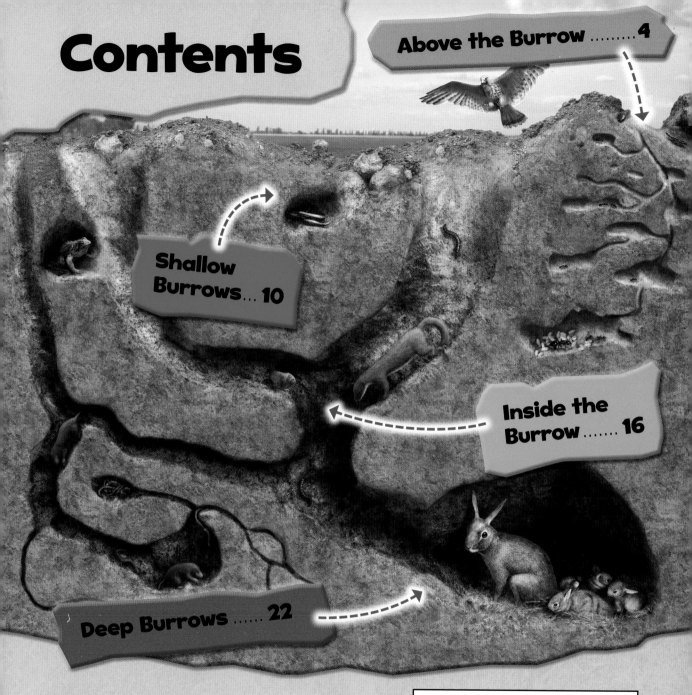

Some words are shown in bold, **like this**. You can find out what they mean by looking in the glossary.

Above the Burrow

Burrows are holes and tunnels dug by animals in the ground. Many animals live in or visit the top of a burrow **habitat**. A habitat is a place that gives animals **shelter** and food.

Slugs are tiny creatures that make **mucus** trails to slide along. They sometimes visit the ground around burrows to feed on animals' poop!

▲ Slugs dig down into the soil from the surface.

A kestrel is a small **bird of prey** that hunts from the air. It flaps its wings to **hover** above burrows where animals might hide. If it sees an animal to eat, it swoops down to catch it.

▼ Kestrels watch burrows closely for animals.

▲ A kestrel has a hook-shaped beak.

Kestrels have large eyes to spot **prey** from high up in the air. They use their sharp claws to grip prey. They eat it by tearing off pieces with their beak.

Earwigs are **insects** with sharp **pincers**. They use these to scare away animals that want to eat them or their young. They also use the pincers to clean themselves.

▼ Earwig pincers can give a painful nip!

pincers

▲ This earwig has found a dead moth to eat.

Many earwigs spend most of the day
hiding in spaces at the tops of old
burrows. They come out at night to
search for rotting plants and animals
to eat.

Shallow Burrows

Many animals live in shallow burrows. Some make their burrows in the loose soil left after other animals dig. Some move into the upper parts of other animals' burrows.

Toads are **amphibians** with bumpy skin. They use the soil around burrows as **shelter** from cold weather. Toads catch slugs and other small animals using their long, sticky tongues.

▲ A toad can flick out its tongue very fast!

Black ants are small **insects** that live in large groups. The ants dig a **nest** together in loose soil. Burrows lead from the surface to the underground spaces where the ants live.

▼ These ants are returning to their burrow.

▲ This ant is carrying food back to its nest.

The queen ant is the biggest ant in the group. She lays eggs in the nest. Worker ants look after her and her baby ants. They fetch food for ants in the nest.

Slow worms are **lizards** that have no legs! They move along on their bellies like snakes. If a **predator** tries to catch a slow worm by its tail, the tail breaks off and the slow worm escapes!

▼ This is a slithering slow worm!

▲ Slow worms can easily slip through soil.

In cold weather, slow worms dig into soil or move into shallow burrows to sleep where it is warmer. They come out to hunt for **prey** such as slugs when it is warm outside.

Inside the Burrow

Different animals spend time inside burrows. Some come to hide or rest. Others are hunting for **prey** to eat.

Voles are small, furry **mammals**. They dig burrows under plants so they can eat the juicy **roots** beneath. Voles also use other animals' burrows for **shelter**.

▲ This vole is nibbling on some grass.

Centipedes are long, flat creatures with many legs. They live in damp, dark places, such as other animals' burrows. Centipedes hunt other tiny creatures, such as slugs, worms, and spiders.

▼ A centipede's many legs help it to move fast!

pincer

▲ Centipedes can look fierce up close!

A centipede has sharp **pincers** behind its head. It uses them to grab **prey** and put **poison** into it. This stops the prey from wriggling while the centipede eats it!

Ermines are long, thin **mammals** with brown backs and a white belly. In snowy places, ermines have white fur all over to help them hide from **predators**, such as hawks.

Ermines stand ▶ up tall so that they can see and smell things better.

▲ Some burrows can be a tight squeeze!

The ermine's long, thin body lets it squeeze down into animal burrows. Ermines hunt for voles and rabbits during the day and night. An ermine bites its **prey** in the neck to kill it before eating it.

Deep Burrows

Some animals dig burrows deep under the ground, where they can find **shelter** and food. Some animals spend all their lives beneath the surface.

Earthworms wriggle through the soil and make narrow burrows as they go. They eat soil as they move so they can get tiny pieces of food from it, such as bits of leaf. Then they poop out the rest.

▲ Earthworms breathe through their skin.

Moles are small **mammals** with brown fur that always live underground. They have tough claws on their front feet to dig their burrows. Molehills are the piles of soil they dig out!

▼ Mole feet are made for digging!

▲ This mole has just found a tasty meal!

Moles look for worms to eat in their burrows. Their noses smell worms, and their whiskers feel them moving along. Moles grab the slippery worms in their sharp teeth before swallowing.

Groups of rabbits dig many different burrows and holes to make their homes. Rabbits use their burrows to hide from **predators**, such as owls. They sleep and have their young in their burrows.

▼ Rabbits come out of their burrows to feed.

▲ These babies are snug in their nest.

A **female** rabbit makes a **nest** in the
burrow from soft fur and grass to keep
her babies warm. She feeds the babies
once a day. Then she blocks the tunnel
with soil to help keep predators out.

Burrow Habitats

Around the world, many different animals live in burrows. Many are small, but some are big. Aardvarks dig burrows up to 43 feet (13 meters) long to rest in during the day and to escape **predators**!

▲ Aardvarks dig burrows in Africa.

▲ Prairie dogs live in burrows in North America.

Burrow **habitats** keep soil healthy by letting air, seeds, and waste into the soil. When soil is healthy, more plants grow. Then more animals can live in the habitat above the burrows.

Glossary

amphibian type of animal that begins life in water and then lives on land for part of its life. Salamanders, frogs, and toads are types of amphibian.

bird of prey bird, such as a hawk or eagle, that hunts animals to eat

female sex of an animal or plant that is able to produce eggs or seeds. Females are the opposite sex to males.

habitat place where particular types of living things are likely to live. For example, polar bears live in snowy habitats and camels live in desert habitats.

hover stay hanging in the air

insect type of small animal that has three body parts, six legs, and usually wings. Ants and dragonflies are types of insect.

lizard type of animal that lives on land and has scales and usually four legs. An iguana is a type of lizard.

mammal animal that has hair and feeds its babies with milk from the mother. Humans and squirrels are types of mammal.

mucus slime

nest place where a bird or other animal lays eggs or cares for its young. Nests are often made from twigs or grass.

pincers body part made of two movable, sharp pieces that can grasp things

poison substance that can harm or kill an animal

predator animal that hunts and catches other animals for food

prey animal that is caught and eaten by another animal

root underground part of a plant that takes in water and useful substances from the soil

shelter place that provides protection from danger or bad weather

Find Out More

Books

Cheshire, Gerard. *Scary Creatures of the Soil* (Scary Creatures). New York: Franklin Watts, 2009.

Miller, Sara Swan. *Secret Lives of Soil Creatures* (Secret Lives). New York: Marshall Cavendish Benchmark, 2010.

Ridley, Sarah. *Minibeasts in the Soil* (Where to Find Minibeasts). Mankato, Minn.: Smart Apple Media, 2010.

Web sites

Facthound offers a safe, fun way to find web sites related to this book. All of the sites on Facthound have been researched by our staff.

Here's all you do:

Visit www.facthound.com

Type in this code: 9781432971939

Index